Table of Contents

Table of Contents

Table of Contents

Table of Contents

Table of Contents

Made in the USA
San Bernardino,
CA

56451212R00089